THE INTERWAR YEARS

The Great Depression

Avery Elizabeth Hurt

Cavendish Square
New York

Published in 2018 by Cavendish Square Publishing, LLC
243 5th Avenue, Suite 136, New York, NY 10016

First Edition

Website: cavendishsq.com

CPSIA Compliance Information: Batch #CS17CSQ

Library of Congress Cataloging-in-Publication Data

Names: Hurt, Avery, author.
Title: The Great Depression / Avery Elizabeth Hurt.
Description: New York : Cavendish Square Publishing, [2018] | Series: The interwar years | Includes bibliographical references and index.
Identifiers: LCCN 2016056412 (print) | LCCN 2016059950 (ebook) | ISBN 9781502627131 (library bound) | ISBN 9781502627148 (E-book)
Subjects: LCSH: United States--History--1933-1945--Juvenile literature. | United States--History--1919-1933--Juvenile literature. | Depressions--1929--United States--Juvenile literature. | New Deal, 1933-1939--Juvenile literature. | United States--Economic conditions--1918-1945--Juvenile literature.
Classification: LCC E806 .H925 2018 (print) | LCC E806 (ebook) | DDC 973.91/6--dc23
LC record available at https://lccn.loc.gov/2016056412

Editorial Director: David McNamara
Editor: Kristen Susienka
Copy Editor: Alex Tessman
Associate Art Director: Amy Greenan
Designer: Alan Sliwinski
Production Coordinator: Karol Szymczuk
Photo Research: J8 Media

The photographs in this book are used by permission and through the courtesy of: Cover, p.1 DEA/A. DAGLI ORTI/De Agostini Picture Library/Getty Images; p. Background Used Throughout james weston/Shutterstock.com; p. Background Used Throughout supermimicry/Shutterstock.com; p. 4 Edward Steichen/Condé Nast via Getty Images; p. 8 f8 archive/Alamy Stock Photo; p. 11, 96 H.Armstrong Roberts/Retrofile/Getty Images; p. 14, 24-25 Everett Historical/Shutterstock.com; p. 16, 29 Universal History Archive/UIG via Getty Images; p. 21 National Photo Company/Wikimedia Commons/File:K.K.K. parade, 1925 npcc 14028.jpg/CC-SA; p. 34 FPG/Hulton Archive/Getty Images; p. 36, 41, 47, 81, 111 Bettmann/Getty Images; p. 39 NY Daily News Archive via Getty Images; p. 49 © CORBIS/Corbis via Getty Images; p. 54 Photoonlife/Shutterstock.com; p. 56 United States Department of Agriculture; Image Number: 00di0971/Wikimedia Commons/File:Dust Bowl Dallas, South Dakota 1936.jpg/CC-SA; p. 60 Al Aumuller/New York World Telegram and the Sun (uploaded by User:Urban)/Wikimedia Commons/File:Woody Guthrie 2.jpg/CC-SA; p. 63 Hulton Archive/Getty Images; p. 67 Walker Evans, for the Farm Security Administration/Office of War Information/Office; p. of Emergency Management/Resettlement Administration/Wikimedia Commons/File:Allie Mae Burroughs print.jpg/CC-SA; p. 71 ullstein bild/ullstein bild via Getty Images; p. 76 David J. & Janice L. Frent/Corbis via Getty Images; p. 84 Charles Russell/Wikimedia Commons/File:Reichsparteitag 1935 Großer Appell 281121M; p. original.jpg/CC-SA; p. 88 Revent/Wikimedia Commons/File:Yalta Conference 1945 Churchill, Stalin, Roosevelt.jpg/CC-SA; p. 92 U.S. Air Force photo/Wikimedia Commons/File:Color Photographed B17E in Flight.jpg/CC-SA; p. 100 Frederic Lewis/Archive Photos/Getty Images; p. 102 Monkey Business/Shutterstock.com; p. 105 MPI/Getty Images.

Printed in the United States of America

Contents

INTRODUCTION

From the Roaring Twenties to the Crash

The first decade after World War I ended in 1918 were years of great prosperity and an almost giddy atmosphere in the United States. Americans had made a lot of sacrifices during the war years, but now that the war had ended, they were ready to have some fun. It seemed like the hard times were over and nothing could go wrong.

Boom Times

After a severe but brief recession at the beginning of the decade, the US economy boomed in the 1920s as the manufacturing industry surged. Cities were growing as more people moved from the countryside to the cities for the new manufacturing jobs. Suddenly there were more things for people to buy—cars, radios, refrigerators, washing machines.

Opposite: *After World War I and before the Great Depression, many Americans enjoyed a time of economic prosperity.*

towns had restrictions on where black people could live. In some places, this had the effect of pushing blacks out of the town. Texas had six towns in which there was nowhere at all for blacks to live. Schools, colleges, and hospitals were segregated throughout the South, and in North Carolina, black and white students used separate schoolbooks. And of course, blacks were not allowed to vote against these laws. The Fifteenth Amendment to the Constitution had given black men the right to vote, but Southern states found ways of denying them that right. Encouraged by court rulings that upheld limits on voting rights, states passed laws saying that only those who owned property could vote, or only those who could read well or whose grandfathers had been able to vote could vote. People were often required to pay a tax at the polls. All these measures served to disenfranchise blacks once again.

As early as 1916, Southern black families had begun moving north to escape racism and find jobs in the factories there. One black man told the *Chicago Daily Tribune*, "I cannot live in North Carolina and be a man and be treated as a man." According to some estimates, between 1915 and 1920 as many as half a million blacks moved to Northern cities, such as Detroit, Chicago, and New York, and between 750,000 and a million blacks left the South in the 1920s. This became known as the Great Migration, and had a profound effect on not just black culture, but the culture of the nation.

Blacks found that racism was not limited to the South. Though discrimination was not as often written into the law in the North, unwritten rules still kept blacks segregated and denied them both rights and dignity. Once the Depression arrived, the economic opportunities evaporated as well. However, the Great Migration caused blacks to form strong bonds and strong communities in their new cities.

The 1920s was a period of great artistic expression for blacks in literature, music, and thought. Since much of

Black sharecroppers in the South did not enjoy the postwar prosperity that many experienced during the Roaring Twenties.

Looking back, it seems obvious that the good times could not last, but at the time, few saw it coming. Nonetheless, in 1929 the US stock market crashed, beginning a cascade of events culminating in an economic catastrophe called the Great Depression that affected the United States and Europe most severely, but left no nation untouched.

By the early 1930s, one out of every four Americans was out of work—roughly one out of four families had no income. People came home to find their belongings piled

People who had lost their homes set up housing wherever they could find a place, like this shantytown on the East River in New York City.

on the sidewalk or front lawns as landlords and banks took possession of what had been their houses. In one single month in 1931, 1,300 families were evicted. Many people moved to vacant lots or railway yards and built makeshift shelters from pieces of tin and packing crates, or whatever bits and pieces of lumber they could scrounge. They stood in long lines at soup kitchens to get something to eat—and they marched on Washington, demanding help. Help did come eventually, in the form of a series of social and economic programs called the New Deal. However, it took a long time for the nation to recover, and it has never been the same since.

The Great Depression lasted for the better part of a decade and changed more than just the economic structure of the country. In fact, some of those changes are still being felt today.

1

Entering the Great Depression

Though historians and economists still do not agree on the exact and immediate causes of the Great Depression, it is clear that much of the trouble that led to the worst economic disaster in US history was caused by the economic policies and conditions that followed World War I (1914–1918).

Triumphs and Trials

The first few years after the end of World War I were prosperous for the United States and, thanks to US investment in the rebuilding of Europe, were somewhat prosperous for Europe as well. In fact, for the United States at least, the 1920s were boom years. However, it was a fragile prosperity. Several factors worked together to weaken the US

Opposite: *In 1919, leaders of the United States, France, and Britain signed the Treaty of Versailles, ending World War I, but following, the United States moved into a dangerous isolationism.*

economy: too much dependence on a few sectors, particularly agriculture and construction; an unequal distribution of wealth resulting in lower demand for goods and increased personal debt; reduced European demand for American goods; low crop prices that made it impossible for farmers to pay bank loans; and banks recklessly investing in the booming stock market. By 1929, the United States economy was in a depression. When the stock market crashed in October, things became significantly worse, beginning what would be the worst and the longest economic catastrophe in the nation's history. The economic disaster soon spread to the rest of the world, and decisions made in the immediate postwar period came back to haunt the victors.

Trouble in Europe

At the end of World War I, the European allies owed lots of money to the United States—far more than they could hope to pay back considering the condition of their economies in the aftermath of the war. In addition, the United States imposed **tariffs**, making it difficult for European countries to sell goods in American markets. The European allies hoped to raise the money to pay off their war debt from war **reparations** imposed on Germany and Austria. That's why the other Allies had insisted on reparations—against the wishes of US president Woodrow Wilson. However, Germany and Austria were in no better position to pay reparations than the European Allies were to pay off war debts. The United States refused to forgive the debt, but American banks were more than willing to loan money to European countries, which the Allies used to pay their war debts. This only created more and unfortunately greater debt. Eventually, the Europeans began to **default** on their loans. The house of cards that began coming down on Wall Street soon crashed all over the European continent. However, much of the trouble was imbedded in the American postwar economy and in how the American attitude influenced that economy.

Slamming the Door

The United States had come to World War I late and reluctantly. For most of its history, it had preferred to stay out of the affairs of other nations when possible and remained carefully neutral for the first few years of the conflict in Europe. However, Germany pursued a policy of sinking merchant ships, and when American travelers were killed by German U-boats, support for the war among Americans increased. Things also were going very badly for the Allies, and they clearly needed help. The United States eventually entered the war on the side of the Allies, but as soon as the war was over, Americans wanted to put that difficult chapter behind them. World War I had been an extremely brutal and traumatic experience for anyone involved in it. Americans tended to see the war as a result of the inability of Europeans to get along with each other. The United States stepped in to help, then wanted to go home and wash their hands of

THE GREAT FLOOD

In 1927, after months of heavy rains and flooding—ten times the yearly average of rainfall—the Mississippi River overflowed its banks and the **levees** couldn't hold. Water poured through the breaks in the levees, covering the land with over 30 feet (9 m) of water. An area roughly the size of Massachusetts, Connecticut, New Hampshire, and Vermont combined was submerged. And still it kept raining. Hundreds of thousands of people were displaced, and at least 250 people died.

Then-president Coolidge appointed Herbert Hoover to organize and oversee a relief effort. Hoover was an engineer by training and had led food relief programs in Europe after World War I. He was the man for the job.

Aftermath of the Mississippi River floods of 1927.

Unfortunately, he had to depend on donations from wealthy philanthropists, and there was not enough money to do what needed to be done. Coolidge was totally opposed to using public funds to help with natural disasters. After a time, however, Congress put together legislation that would provide aid for the flooded communities. Coolidge still resisted. Eventually they struck a deal for some rather stingy relief. Though this aid was nothing like what the government was soon to do in the wake of the Great Depression and was not nearly enough to meet the needs of the communities affected by the floods, it was a first step in setting expectations that the government might play a role in helping citizens after disasters.

Both men who served as president during the 1920s, Warren G. Harding and Calvin Coolidge, were unspectacular leaders. Harding served from 1921 until August 1923 when he died suddenly of a heart attack. Coolidge, his vice president, stepped in and served until 1929. Both men were weak leaders who left a lot of government work to party officials and cabinet members. Coolidge was even less interested in governing than Harding had been, particularly when it came to the economy. He believed that the government should play as little role as possible in the affairs of the nation—especially its economic affairs. Nonetheless, much of the rest of the federal government spent these years working hard to support the success of business and industry. Corporate taxes and inheritance taxes were greatly reduced and government spending was cut dramatically. The secretary of commerce, Herbert Hoover, strongly believed that economic stability could be achieved by business leaders in the private sector working together voluntarily. He encouraged trade associations in which similar businesses cooperated—not to fix prices but to increase production and marketing efficiency.

Meanwhile, the Supreme Court continued to weaken the rights of workers, striking down a law that limited the numbers of hours bakers could be required to work, reversing the few existing federal child labor protections and minimum wage laws, and upholding laws that attempted to put restraints on trade or business practices. Business and industry were making money, and the government was willing to support that in whatever way they could—even if at the expense of large segments of society and at the risk of creating dangerous corporate monopolies. Some progressives in Congress were worried about the government's close ties with business and tried to introduce legislation to help farmers and use federal funds for public works, such as electric power projects on the Tennessee River. However, they did not have enough support in Congress to get these measures through. If the United States was stingy with Europe, it was equally stingy at home. Public spending, including spending at state and local levels, was only a small fraction of the **gross domestic product (GDP)**. This meant that the government was not investing in its own economy, and it put the federal government in a very weak position for dealing with the Great Depression when it finally arrived. In the long run, these policies were disastrous. By considering only the interests of business and assuming that what was good for business was good for the nation, the federal government had designed a system for which failure was inevitable.

For a while it seemed as if none of this mattered. In the first few years after the end of the war, the US economy was on fire. Factories were putting people to work churning out consumer goods, and people were snapping these goods up on the installment plan or other forms of credit. It seemed like an economic miracle. In fact, economically things *were* pretty good during the 1920s—at least on the surface. Manufacturing output rose by 60 percent and per capita income increased by one-third. The burgeoning automobile industry created opportunities for related industries—steel, rubber, glass, and tools—to flourish as well. And with all those cars around, road construction thrived too. When people had cars, they could drive into the city for work, so they bought houses in the suburbs, creating opportunities in the home construction business. In addition, there were many new industries, thanks to technological innovations: electronics, home appliances, aviation, and even the new film industry. Even though not all Americans enjoyed the success of these boom years and despite its underlying fragility, the US economy did seem to be doing very well.

Money Machine

The US Stock Exchange also enjoyed tremendous growth during the 1920s. Between 1921 and 1929, the value of the stock market increased by 600 percent. Investment in the stock market grew faster than the actual production of consumer goods, and the stocks people were buying and selling were priced higher than the actual value of the companies they represented. Previously, people had bought stocks as a long-term investment in the economy of the country, but by the end of the 1920s, it had become a way for people to make a lot of money fast, with no commitment to the long-term prospects of the businesses in which they were investing. It seemed to many as if the stock market were a money machine, spitting out profits like a factory assembly line turning out washing machines—and it looked like a way for Americans to get rich quick. They bought stock in

In the years before the stock market crash of 1929, many people bought and sold stocks recklessly.

companies that were expected to make a huge profit—often by selling goods on credit—and then watched carefully as the stock prices rose. Then they sold the stock for a nice profit before the value began to come down again. People even borrowed money to buy stocks (something called buying "on margin"), planning to pay off that debt when the stock rose and they cashed in. What they didn't realize was that the economy that underpinned the stock market was in serious

Crash!

By the fall of 1929, investors were worried about the market. They realized that it was only a matter of time before the stocks they had invested in lost value. Everyone was jittery about when to sell. Over several days in October of that year, prices started to fall and investors began selling out, only causing prices to fall further. Because so many people had borrowed money to buy stocks, they had to sell quickly when the prices started dropping so that they would be able to get enough money to back their loans. This only increased the pace of the sell-offs and reduced prices further. On Tuesday, October 29, 1929, prices completely collapsed. Between ten and fifteen billion dollars were lost on that one day, forever remembered as Black Tuesday. While many individual investors lost money, businesses were heavily invested in the market as well, and this caused a great deal of ongoing damage to the economy.

The stock market crash of 1929 did not cause the Great Depression. As we have seen, the economy was already in serious trouble and the crash was more a symptom than a cause. However, it did set off a chain of events that sent an already shaky economy over the edge. After the crash, the rest of the economy rapidly unraveled. The uncertainty sparked by the implosion of the stock market caused people to spend less money, which meant that companies sold fewer goods and had to shut down production and let go of workers, or at the very least cut back on workers' hours. This, of course,

JUMPERS ON WALL STREET

An October 30, 1929, article in the *New York Daily News* described how the homes and life savings of many investors were lost in a matter of hours on October 29. Men and women who had put all their savings into the stock market so that they could live comfortably in retirement quite suddenly found that they had nothing.

There were rumors at the time that desperate investors by the dozens were leaping to their deaths from the high-rise buildings on Wall Street. An article in a London tabloid reported that the street was clogged with corpses. Humorist Will Rogers joked, "When Wall Street took that tail spin, you had to stand in line to get a window to jump out of."

A bit of *schadenfreude* over wealthy speculators getting what many people thought they deserved may have been behind these sensational reports. While the situation was grim and the despair was real, people weren't leaping to their deaths in droves. According to data collected by the *New York Times*, between October 24, 1929, and the end of that year, only eight people jumped to their deaths, and only four of those suicides could be attributed to the stock market crash. Two were on Wall Street. There is no doubt that many lives were ruined that day and the despair was real, but the popular image of investors leaping out of windows and bodies piling up on the street is just a myth.

Crowds of depositors arrive to find their banks have gone bankrupt virtually overnight after the stock market collapse.

meant people had less money to spend. Demand for goods dropped even more, probably because people were shaken about the economy and unwilling to make major purchases until things looked better. Even people who still had jobs and perhaps some savings felt insecure about the state of the economy and not in a mood to spend freely. It was a downward spiral. The GDP of the United States dropped 25 percent in three years.

The banking system almost totally collapsed in the wake of the crash. More than nine thousand American banks either closed or went bankrupt between 1930 and 1933. With so many banks failing, people rushed to their banks to withdraw their money, only to find that their savings or deposits they'd thought were being safely kept in the bank had been invested in the stock market or loaned to someone else. The bank didn't actually have their money. Many people who did have a bit of cash after the crash were reluctant to put it in banks, keeping what cash they had on hand instead.

Not only did the Great Depression put millions of people out of work and in poverty, but it shook the nation's faith in its entire economic and political system. Almost no institution in the nation's economy was reliable any longer. People began to question whether the capitalist system the United States was founded on was even workable.

Though there were plenty of signs that the economy was headed for trouble, few people saw it coming. When it did happen, it occurred so suddenly and so dramatically that the population and the nation's leaders were stunned. It took a while to sort through things and decide how to respond. Over the next few years, the public and politicians alike worked not only to figure out how to repair the economy but also to repair the badly shaken faith of the American people. However, things would get much worse before they began to get better.

2

A New Deal for the Nation

At first the nation's leaders put up an optimistic front and tried to reassure people that everything would be fine. President Herbert Hoover (former Commerce Secretary) had been inaugurated as president in March 1929. He was the third Republican in a row to be elected president; it seemed that the voters were happy with the government's policies, and Hoover saw no reason to change them. He told the public that the downturn in the economy, which he called a "depression" rather than using the then-common term "panic" or "crisis," was a normal part of the ups and downs of free market economies and that they had nothing to fear. Indeed, the country had been through several depressions in the 1800s and had come out of each of them relatively quickly.

Opposite: *President Hoover tried to reassure a worried nation that the economic downturn was temporary and mild.*

Meanwhile, he called on the leaders of industry to continue as much production as possible, maintain wages, and keep a lid on labor conflicts, though other than continuing to block unions in whatever way they could, there was not much businesses were willing or able to do. Hoover was staunchly opposed to the government helping in any way with individual problems. He expected neighbors to help neighbors and individuals and local governments to bear the responsibility for taking care of the millions of Americans left homeless and hungry through no fault of their own. In a radio address to the nation in 1931, Hoover told a population desperate for help, "No governmental action, no economic doctrine, no economic plan or project can replace that God-imposed responsibility of the individual man and woman to their neighbors."

That is not to say that Hoover did nothing. He did take some action—much of which actually made the situation worse. In 1930, he signed the Smoot-Hawley Tariff Act, which significantly raised already high tariffs on goods imported from other nations prompting retaliatory measures, once again slamming the door on the rest of the world, and at a time when the United States desperately needed to trade with other nations. Then in 1931, the **Federal Reserve** raised interest rates, which further reduced the amount of money in circulation. With less ability to borrow, businesses were unable to do as Hoover had asked and keep up production, forcing them to lay off more workers, which in turn reduced demand even further. With the economy getting worse by the

There was nothing funny about having to live in a Hooverville, like this one in New York City's Central Park.

day, investors began to pull their money out of US businesses, only making things worse. It seemed as if there were no way to stop the downward spiral.

President Hoover became increasingly unpopular. People who had lost their jobs and homes began to refer to the makeshift communities in railroad yards as "Hoovervilles." "Hoover flags" were empty pants pockets turned inside-out. The newspapers people covered themselves with to stay warm when they slept outside were called "Hoover blankets." By the time the 1932 election rolled around, American voters had had enough of Hoover, the Republican Party, and their policies of helping business but letting individuals tough it out.

Facing a tough reelection campaign, Hoover finally began to offer a little federal help—not to individuals but to stimulate banks and businesses, hoping to boost the economy from the top. He authorized an agency, the Reconstruction Finance Corporation, that would give loans to banks, railroads, and insurance companies, hoping that these companies would use the money in a way that would trickle down to the people who were suffering. Mostly, however, these banks used the funds to replace their own lost assets rather than lending the money to businesses that might use them to pay workers. After this plan failed miserably, Hoover backed construction programs for government buildings and other public construction projects as a way of putting people to work. However, this was too little and too late to have more than a very small impact on an economy in free fall.

A New Leader

Franklin Delano Roosevelt, the governor of New York, ran for president on the Democratic ticket in 1932. He campaigned on promises of better times but did not mention many details about how he planned to improve the economy and put people back to work. He did make it clear, though, that he intended for the federal government to play a major role in reviving the economy. He talked about taking care of "the forgotten man," and offered a "new deal" for the country. He defeated Hoover in a landslide.

Franklin Roosevelt had no problem convincing a desperate nation to give him a chance to lead the United States out of its troubles.

By the time Roosevelt took office, things had gotten even worse. Between 1929 and 1932 an average of one hundred thousand workers lost their jobs *each week*. By inauguration day in March 1933, 25 percent of the workforce was out of a job; industrial production was half what it had been before the Depression began; farmers were unable to sell their crops, while people in the cities went hungry because they couldn't afford groceries; and banks were continuing to fail. The new president had a lot of work to do—and he got busy doing it.

The most pressing issue was the banking crisis. Two days after being sworn into office, Roosevelt declared a national

Shame of Poverty

Hoover's attitude toward the poor—that it was the responsibility of families and the community and most certainly *not* the government to take care of them, if they were taken care of at all—was harsh, but it wasn't unusual. Prior to the Great Depression, most Americans had similar ideas. One reason Americans were never very keen on helping others in need was an old, perhaps often subconscious, belief that success was something one earned; therefore, if someone wasn't successful it was because they hadn't worked hard enough. In essence, the poor deserved their fate. When the economy was booming and jobs were plentiful (or were plentiful if you were white, male, healthy, and had the skills to work in some of these new jobs on assembly lines), it was easy for a lot of people to believe that those who did not have jobs just weren't trying hard enough.

Of course, people who had attitudes like these found it especially hard to lose their jobs and not be able to find other jobs. Often they blamed themselves and felt a great deal of shame and responsibility for a situation they had no control over. Once assistance became available, some people found it very hard to accept it. When they finally did go for help, people told stories of having waited weeks, living on bread and water, before breaking down and registering for relief. The shame of joblessness was so intense for some people that they withdrew from society and stayed home, hoping to keep what they considered their failure a secret. That was

Franklin Roosevelt had no problem convincing a desperate nation to give him a chance to lead the United States out of its troubles.

By the time Roosevelt took office, things had gotten even worse. Between 1929 and 1932 an average of one hundred thousand workers lost their jobs *each week*. By inauguration day in March 1933, 25 percent of the workforce was out of a job; industrial production was half what it had been before the Depression began; farmers were unable to sell their crops, while people in the cities went hungry because they couldn't afford groceries; and banks were continuing to fail. The new president had a lot of work to do—and he got busy doing it.

The most pressing issue was the banking crisis. Two days after being sworn into office, Roosevelt declared a national banking holiday and closed all the banks that were still in business in the country. Then three days later, he signed the Emergency Banking Act, making these closures legal. The Emergency Banking Act also authorized the Federal Reserve to loan money to these banks so that they could reopen with enough cash to actually cover the money people had deposited in them. The treasury department examined and certified banks as solvent before they were allowed to reopen. Troubled banks were either given assistance or closed for good if they were beyond hope. Roosevelt assured the public that it was now safer to put their money back in the bank than to keep it under the mattress. Moreover, he explained why doing that would help to restore the economy. The people had faith in him. The next morning, people who had rushed to the bank to withdraw their money rushed back to redeposit it.

A Flood of Legislation

With the banking crisis solved, Roosevelt turned his attention to getting people back to work. The New Deal he promised had three parts: relief, recovery, and reform. Relief to help people who were suffering, recovery to get the economy back on track, and reform to keep this kind of disaster from happening again.

One reason candidate Roosevelt had been short on specifics about how he planned to repair the economy was that he didn't have a specific plan. His approach was more experimental. He tried things and if they didn't work, he ditched them and tried something else. This was no time to stick with a philosophy or ideology just because you believed in it. In his first few months in office, he pushed through fifteen major pieces of legislation—relief programs, farm bills, banking reform. Much of this legislation created what came to be called an "alphabet soup" of federal agencies because so many of them were known by their initials.

The AAA was the Agricultural Adjustment Act, designed to solve the farm crisis, but to many it seemed like a ridiculous, even dangerous, thing to do. It created a federal agency that would pay farmers not to grow crops or raise animals. Overproduction of farm crops was one of the factors that caused prices to drop so dramatically, impoverishing farmers. Reducing the amount of crops produced was expected to increase prices. In January 1936, the Supreme Court ruled the AAA unconstitutional on the grounds that it was an abuse of the government's taxing authority. However, farm subsidies are still around today. Another agency, the National Recovery Administration (NRA), was meant to do something similar for industry by allowing the federal government to regulate production and wages. The Supreme Court declared the NRA unconstitutional as well.

A Nation Gets Back Work

Not all of Roosevelt's programs were shot down by the courts. Young men were hit especially hard by the employment crisis. The Civilian Conservation Corps (CCC) was created during

Roosevelt's first one hundred days in office. The Corps hired young men to work draining swamps, building dams, and planting trees in the national parks. These young men lived in barracks and sent their wages home to their families. They could enlist in the program for up to two years.

In 1935, Congress passed the Emergency Relief Appropriations Act. This bit of legislation gave the president almost five billion dollars to support pretty much any program that might help the recovery. Most of the money was used for the Works Progress Administration (WPA). This was by far the biggest jobs program of the New Deal. Over the course of eight years, the program hired 8.5 million people to build bridges, schools, parks, and airports; repair library books, sew clothes; and index newspapers. The WPA employed far more men than women but paid women the same as men for the same work. Even so, women were typically employed in lower-paying jobs. The program also found work for artists and writers and musicians; Saul Bellow and Richard Wright were hired to write guidebooks for each of the fifty states, while other writers collected folktales and local stories. Actors performed stage plays and puppet shows. Photographers, such as Dorothea Lange and Walker Evans, traveled the country, documenting life in America during the Depression. Though it was more expensive to provide jobs than to just hand out relief checks (though 90 percent of the budget was spent on labor and only 10 percent on materials and administration), the advantages to the morale of the country were impressive. As Harry Hopkins, the director of the WPA, put it, "Give a man a dole, and you save his body and destroy his spirit. Give him a job, and you save both body and spirit."

The National Labor Relations Act (or the Wagner Act) was also passed in 1935. It established the National Labor Relations Board, which could impose sanctions on businesses that engaged in unfair labor practices. This resulted in an immediate and dramatic increase in union membership.

Soon after the National Labor Relations Act was passed, Congress took up the issue of living conditions for the elderly. The nation had never had any provisions for people who were no longer able to work. If old people had no savings and no families to care for them, they were forced into poverty. Robert Wagner, the same senator who had sponsored the National Labor Relations/Wagner Act, sponsored the Social Security Bill. This legislation was signed into law on August 14, 1935, creating a social insurance program that paid retired workers over the age of sixty-five a small regular income. It did not provide medical coverage for retired people (that would have to wait until 1965 and Lyndon Johnson's Great Society Program), but it did provide support for disabled workers and poor mothers and their children, establishing some social programs that would last well beyond the end of the Depression (though the Wagner Act was severely limited by later legislation).

Resistance

The success of the WPA was in many ways a high point of Roosevelt's programs. As his first term wore on, he began to encounter more resistance—from both the right and the left of the political spectrum. The corporate world, especially, began to distrust and oppose him. He was accused of reckless spending and socialist reforms. Rather than slowing him down, however, this criticism only convinced him that there was no use making compromises to please them, and he should just go on regardless with what he thought was best. In his campaign for reelection in 1936, he said that what he called the forces of organized money "are unanimous in their hate for me—and I welcome their hatred."

Perhaps more surprisingly, Roosevelt also got some criticism from the left. Many criticized him at times for not going far enough. One alternative plan, touted by Senator Huey Long of Louisiana, was based on the belief that the main economic problem was the unequal distribution of wealth. Long's plan was to allow no individual to have more than fifty million dollars (or possibly less, depending on the needs of society) and to redistribute any wealth beyond that to the public through benefits and public works. Long believed it was immoral for anyone to live in poverty when there was enough wealth in the nation to provide the necessities for everyone. Long was dismissed in the press, but he went directly to the people via speaking engagements, radio addresses, and his own newspaper, and garnered a great deal of support. This

People like Huey Long of Louisiana pushed Roosevelt even further to the left of the political spectrum.

forced Roosevelt to embrace an even more liberal agenda for his New Deal. Programs like the WPA, the NLRB, and Social Security may have been due in part to Long's influence. None of these reforms suddenly ended the Depression, but they alleviated a great deal of the suffering.

Shame of Poverty

Hoover's attitude toward the poor—that it was the responsibility of families and the community and most certainly *not* the government to take care of them, if they were taken care of at all—was harsh, but it wasn't unusual. Prior to the Great Depression, most Americans had similar ideas. One reason Americans were never very keen on helping others in need was an old, perhaps often subconscious, belief that success was something one earned; therefore, if someone wasn't successful it was because they hadn't worked hard enough. In essence, the poor deserved their fate. When the economy was booming and jobs were plentiful (or were plentiful if you were white, male, healthy, and had the skills to work in some of these new jobs on assembly lines), it was easy for a lot of people to believe that those who did not have jobs just weren't trying hard enough.

Of course, people who had attitudes like these found it especially hard to lose their jobs and not be able to find other jobs. Often they blamed themselves and felt a great deal of shame and responsibility for a situation they had no control over. Once assistance became available, some people found it very hard to accept it. When they finally did go for help, people told stories of having waited weeks, living on bread and water, before breaking down and registering for relief. The shame of joblessness was so intense for some people that they withdrew from society and stayed home, hoping to keep what they considered their failure a secret. That was

Many people didn't realize how bad the economic situation was until they saw the long lines at food kitchens, like this one.

one reason people who hadn't lost their jobs sometimes didn't realize how many other people had.

Unemployment, though widespread, was not evenly distributed. The young, the old, the uneducated or unskilled, and rural Americans were hit harder than most. Blacks, Mexican-Americans, and immigrants were hit the hardest. One-fifth of the people on the federal relief roles were black, and most of these lived in the rural South. Black unemployment was twice that of white unemployment. The typical unemployed urban worker was a thirty-eight-year-old white man with little education who was head of his household. Before losing his job, he was an unskilled or semiskilled worker in the manufacturing industry.

As the Depression worsened, the destitution became hard to hide. Private charities and state relief programs were overwhelmed. The lines for food at Salvation Army and Red Cross soup kitchens stretched for blocks. People who had lost their homes lived in packing crates and makeshift tents in shantytowns; they dug through garbage cans looking for discarded food or hung around the back doors of restaurants in case the employees passed out leftovers at the end of the evening. Many people in rural America wandered from town to town, hoping that in the next one they would find work. Some climbed into empty railcars and road trains across the country, in case times were better somewhere else. The poor were no longer invisible, and with one-fourth of the population out of work, if you weren't unemployed, you knew someone who was. It finally became obvious in the most painful way that the unemployed and the poor, weren't lazy or losers, they were people just like everyone else, but people who had had some very bad luck. And just maybe, it was the responsibility of the government to do something about it.

That such extensive social programs as Roosevelt implemented, like the WPA and Social Security, were accepted, even welcomed, by the public reflects a deep change

Keynesian Economics—Who Influenced Whom?

John Maynard Keynes was a British economist and the father of the school of thought named after him: Keynesian economics. In 1919, Keynes published *The Economic Consequences of the Peace*, which argued that the excessive reparations imposed on Germany by the Allies would be impossible to repay, and would not only keep Germany in poverty, but politically unstable as well. Then as unemployment in Britain surged to 20 percent during the years between the wars, Keynes developed a somewhat radical theory of economics, which he described in his 1936 book, *The General Theory of Employment, Interest, and Money*. This work completely revolutionized the way economists thought about the causes of and responses to economic downturns and unemployment. Among other things, Keynes argued that full employment could be maintained only by government spending. He advocated **deficit** spending during economic downturns, saying that governments should invest in public works and provide jobs for the unemployed. At the time, balanced budgets were economic orthodoxy, and Keynes's ideas were greeted with a great deal of skepticism. However, policymakers in the United States were looking for ideas—and Keynes's *General Theory* was put to the test.

It has often been said that Roosevelt used Keynes's philosophy as a template for the New Deal. However, Roosevelt himself showed little interest in economic theory, though many of his economic advisors were no doubt more interested in academic economic discussions. In any case, Keynes's *General Theory* wasn't published until 1936—three years after Roosevelt's first one hundred days of stimulus legislation. However, Keynes did write an open letter to President Roosevelt, which was published in the *New York Times* in December 1933, largely endorsing the New Deal. Perhaps the success of the New Deal helped influence Keynes's thinking as much as his thinking influenced the New Deal.

AMERICANS ON THE MOVE

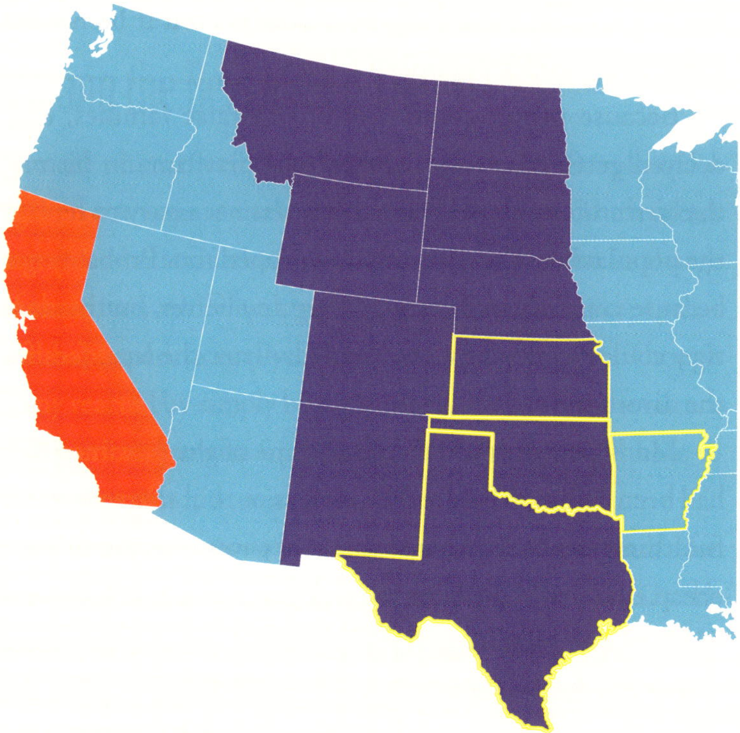

- **1930** Population of California is 5.7 million residents; 120,000 Mexicans repatriated, bringing California's population down.

- **1930s** 2.5 million people left the plains states.

- **1940** Dust farmers totaling 250,000 arrive in California from Oklahoma, Arkansas, Texas, and Kansas.

designed to teach players about the dangers of monopolies and point out the immortality of income inequality. A game that began as a critique of American greed eventually became a celebration of it.)

Movies were popular too and still fairly inexpensive. The first "talkie," a movie with sound as well as pictures, had been produced in 1927, and movies were for the first time being filmed in color. Some of the movies people watched in the 1930s, like *The Wonderful Wizard of Oz,* are still popular today.

The most popular leisure activity during the Great Depression was reading books and magazines, followed by listening to the radio. Americans had fascinating new music to listen to and books to read. The radio especially became a news outlet and entertainment center of family life. Indeed, the Depression changed American culture in all kinds of fascinating ways.

3

Culture in Times of Want

With the exception of the Civil War, no event in American history has had a greater effect on the character of the nation than the Great Depression. Everything from the music people listened to to the books they read, from the way they thought about women or treated African and Mexican Americans was affected and often changed by the economic catastrophe of the Great Depression.

Jazz after the Jazz Age

By the 1930s, most Americans had radios. The price of radios dropped significantly during that time, making it possible for all but the most destitute to have one. People who had bought most of their household goods on credit might have lost

Opposite: *The almost decade-long drought that led to the Dust Bowl left much of the Great Plains in ruins and destroyed many family farms.*

their washing machines and their cars because they couldn't make the payments, but if there was any way they could hang on to the radio, they did. Radios were important for more than just entertainment. President Roosevelt broadcast regular informal addresses, which he called fireside chats. These conversations kept everyone up to date on his policies and programs—and often kept them encouraged as well. However, people didn't just listen to politics and policy—they also listened to music.

The Depression hit the music industry hard. When people could no longer afford to buy records or go to clubs, many musicians found themselves out of work. Some of the big-name musicians, particularly big city band leaders like Duke Ellington and Benny Goodman, continued to do well during the Depression, but for others, times were hard. In the 1920s, people had mostly enjoyed jazz in dance halls and at clubs, and in big cities people still did. But it was harder for people in smaller cities and towns or in the country to hear music in person, especially when so few bands could afford to tour. Fortunately, jazz musicians discovered the power of radio to build audiences. Many big bands sponsored live radio shows, and people around the country tuned in faithfully.

Jazz music had so much defined the 1920s that another term for the era is the Jazz Age, but in the 1930s, this new and completely American form of music changed and became even more representative of the nation. The 1930s was the swing era of jazz. Swing is a type of jazz that is fast and upbeat and optimistic. It's for dancing. However, no matter how fast people danced or how joyful the beat, jazz was never a superficial tonic for easing the pain of the Depression. Jazz had its roots in blues, and jazz was a quintessentially American music, giving voice to the moods of a troubled nation. Jazz standards of the 1930s, like "Mood Indigo" and "Georgia On My Mind," speak to the wistfulness and anguish of the age.

In an article in the *New Republic,* essayist and critic Albert Murray describes jazz this way:

> "*Jazz as such began as a secular dance music that evolved from ragtime piano music, brass-band music, and the guitar, vocal, harmonica, barroom, honky-tonk, and juke-joint music called the blues, which generates an atmosphere of groovy delight and festive well-being in the very process of recounting a tale of woe.*"

Could there be a more perfect form of music for the Great Depression? Jazz matured from the gaudy background music of the giddy 1920s to a hopeful yet clear-eyed soundtrack of the 1930s.

Woody Guthrie's songs, with their often-subversive lyrics, have become part of the United States' shared culture.

Woody Guthrie: Voice of the Dust Bowl

While jazz musicians were filling dance halls in the cities and broadcasting across the nation, another kind of music could be heard in the heartland, and one person more than any other sang the songs that gave a voice to the suffering of ordinary Americans. Woody Guthrie was born in Oklahoma, but by the 1930s he had joined the flow of workers traveling around the country looking for work. Woody was more singer than farmer, and he entertained and documented the American working class in Hoovervilles around the country, particularly in the Midwest and West. He wrote thousands of songs, and his ballads gave voice to the economic distress as well as the courage, resilience, and humor of the American people. He wrote of the heartbreak of losing one's home, of the sorry treatment of union workers at the hands of their bosses, and of the suffering of Mexican migrant workers. He also wrote funny, satirical songs that poked fun at bankers and politicians—and the people he sang with and for sorely needed a bit of humor.

Woody and many of his fans had left the Midwest looking for work after a disaster within a disaster. The economy was bad enough in the 1930s, but on top of that, farmers had to deal with the worst drought in the history of the Great Plains. It lasted most of the decade.

The American plains had originally been covered with grasses, but when farmers settled the area, they plowed deep into the ground to plant crops, or they raised cattle that trampled the native grasses and damaged the soil structure. The region frequently has big windstorms. Without the native grasses to hold the drought-parched soil in place, those storms whipped up huge clouds of dust that raged across the prairie. The sky would be dark for days, and no matter how tightly people sealed their homes, dust would get in and leave thick layers over everything. Nineteen states in the heartland of the country were turned into a giant dust bowl during the 1930s.

It was impossible for farmers to make a living, so many of them abandoned their farms and headed to California, hoping to find work on the big farms there. It's hard to imagine how difficult this decision must have been—to leave your home and farm, often the farm you or your parents had homesteaded—but there seemed no alternative. People had heard that California was the promised land. They'd seen advertisements that promised high wages picking oranges and peaches or gathering grapes. Many families had to sell almost everything they owned to even be able to afford the gas to get out West. Then when they arrived, they discovered that there was not enough work to go around. A farmer who had advertised that he needed a hundred workers might arrive at the fields one morning and find a thousand men (and women and children), hungry and desperate for work.

Many of them were nearly starved by the time they arrived in California, and with no jobs to be had, they had nowhere to go. They set up migrant camps, where they lived crowded into tents and makeshift structures. The travails of these Dust Bowl migrants were inspiration for some of the greatest literature of the period.

Telling the Stories

In the 1920s books like F. Scott Fitzgerald's *The Great Gatsby* and *This Side of Paradise* chronicled the glitz and glamour of the Roaring Twenties, but during the Great Depression, writers turned their attention from the excesses of the wealthy

Langston Hughes was the first poet to use jazz rhythms and black dialect in his work.

to struggles of the poor, and very often to the politics of the era. In a *New York Times* review of *The Grapes of Wrath,* Peter Monro Jack says that the authors of this period are "writing stories and scenarios of America with a curious and sudden intensity, almost as if they had never seen or understood it before. They are looking at it again with revolutionary eyes."

John Steinbeck's *The Grapes of Wrath,* published in 1939, is probably the most well-known novel of the period. Steinbeck tells the story of the Joad family as they head west from the Dust Bowl in search of work after their Oklahoma farm has been repossessed by the bank. Steinbeck wrote a very realistic and deeply disturbing account of the sufferings of the Joad family, while simultaneously offering a strong and moving condemnation of the social and political situation that led to their circumstances. Steinbeck alternates chapters between what he called the particular and the general, the story of the Joads interspersed with chapters that explain as well as evoke the larger historical and social setting of the novel. Steinbeck wrote:

> "*This you may say of man—when theories change and crash, when schools, philosophies, when narrow dark allies of thought, national, religious, economic, grow and disintegrate, man reaches, stumbles forward, painfully, mistakenly, sometimes. Having stepped forward, he may slip back, but only half a step, never the full step back. This you may say and know it and know it.*"

Other writers of this period also used unusual narrative techniques. John Dos Passos's 1936 novel *The Big Money* alternates conventional storytelling with collages of newspaper headlines, lyrics from popular songs, and biographies of people who were influential at the time, to examine many of the causes of the Great Depression. In Dos Passos's telling, "big money" is more of a curse than a blessing. His fictional

ART IN EUROPE

Historian Philipp Blom describes Europe in the 1930s as a "time of broken hope … when the hope of escaping the dynamic of the first world war was finally broken by the world economic crisis." Because World War I was fought in Europe and America was in the war only a short time, Europeans were far more affected by it, and more aware of how senseless the war had been. By the end of the 1920s, European economies were improving and people were becoming more optimistic, and then in 1929 the hope for a better world collapsed along with the world economy.

European art and literature of the interwar period reflects not only the despair created by the Great Depression but by the ravages of war. World War I had featured new and horrible weaponry. Men were not fighting other men as much as they were fighting machines and checmicals—tanks, artillery cannons, mustard gas. In addition to the many people who were killed, many lost limbs or were permanently disfigured.

The artistic and literary movement known as Dada began in Zurich, Switzerland, as a reaction to the horrors of World War I and condemnation of the **nationalism** and social disintegration that led to the war. Dada was the first art movement to focus not on making lovely works of art but on making art that questioned the assumptions of society. Hans (also known as Jean) Arp, Marcel Duchamp, Max Ernst, and Joan Miro were famous Dada artists.

of over eighty thousand images by photographers such as Walker Evans, Ben Shahn, and Arthur Rothstein.

Some of the most heartwrenching photographs were of unemployed men and suffering farmers taken by Dorothea Lange. Before the Depression, Lange had been a professional portrait photographer in San Francisco, California. Her subjects were often successful and wealthy people. When the Depression hit, she turned her camera on the homeless and hungry waiting in bread lines in her city. Her work came to the attention of the FSA, and the agency hired her to travel throughout the West and Southwest, taking portraits that would show the nation just how bad things were for the rural poor. In 1936, on her way home from a month on the road, Lange stopped at a migrant camp and took what is probably the most iconic photograph of the Great Depression. It has come to be known as *Migrant Mother.* A young mother is huddled with three of her children in a rough, makeshift tent. The two older children's faces are buried in their mother's shoulder, and the baby is just barely visible in her blankets. The mother is looking a bit away from the camera, the worry and strain etched into her face. The image is one of despair, and speaks more eloquently than any words of what the Great Depression had done to people. Not only did this image and many others like it show the rest of America the extent of the misery. It provided a lasting record for future generations.

Lange spent much of the rest of her life using her camera to document social injustice. She was a major influence on portrait photography in the years to come.

COMMUNISM

The Communist Party in the United States (CPUSA) was formed in 1919. The rising wealth of the industrial class and the lopsided distribution of wealth that became apparent in the 1920s was a strong recruiting tool for a political party that fought against inequality and the exploitation of workers. However, it was a relatively small movement in the United States, and at the time very much tied to the Communist Party in Moscow.

At first it met with a great deal of resistance from the general public. Americans had always been committed to a free-market **capitalism**, and most Americans shared Hoover's and the Republican Party's insistence on individual self-sufficiency with no help from the government.

Roosevelt's New Deal, however, while by no means eliminating capitalism, certainly sanded off many of its rough edges by using the power and purse of the federal government to adjust and tinker with the economy. Some of Roosevelt's opponents on the right feared the New Deal was going too far toward a communist government. Communists, however, at first resisted these efforts and worked for their own types of reforms. By 1935, though, the US communist movement supported most of Roosevelt's programs. They also coordinated with unions, civil rights organizations, and organizations that defended the rights of immigrants.

Many Americans, experiencing the disastrous results of unfettered capitalism, were sympathetic to the aims of the Communist Party, and CPUSA membership increased by some sixty-five thousand new members during the 1930s. Many Americans agreed with the goals and ideals of the Communist Party but never joined. These people were called "fellow travelers."

Mixed Times for Women

Women had just got the right to vote in 1920, and the following decade had been heady years for the women's movement. Women had cut their hair into short styles called bobs, raised the hemlines of their skirts, and were waiting longer to get married, often working as secretaries or shop clerks for a few years and saving some money before starting a family. Though most women still saw marriage and motherhood as their career, women now seemed to have more options. But after the Great Depression arrived, things changed for women as much as they did for the men who made up most of the workforce.

The Great Depression had a somewhat contradictory effect on attitudes about women. In one way, it reinforced the belief that women belonged in the home and not in the workforce. With so few jobs, it seemed, men should get first shot at them. On the other hand, because so many people were desperate for money, many women—married and not—worked when they could find jobs. By the end of the Depression, 25 percent more women were working than had been before the Depression began.

This doesn't mean women found it easy to join the workforce. Jobs were hard to come by, of course, and men were now taking jobs that in the past were considered jobs for women, such as teaching and social work. Women who worked in industry were more likely than men to be laid off or have their hours or wages—or both—cut. In addition, in order to help more people, the National Industrial Recovery Act made it illegal for two members of the same family to have government jobs. On the other hand, men were less likely to compete with women for the nonprofessional jobs women had always worked, jobs as secretaries, sales clerks, and domestic servants. Some factory owners preferred to hire women for assembly-line work because they could pay women less. Often these jobs required women to work long hours—sometimes as many as fifty hours a week. People were too desperate for jobs to complain, but this was very hard

Frances Perkins, the first woman to serve as a cabinet secretary, is credited with helping create the modern middle class.

HE SAVED AMERICA

4

A Crisis to End a Crisis

The Great Depression was the most serious economic crisis that the United States had ever experienced—and it seemed like it would never end. Historians and economists don't agree on an exact date for the end of the Depression, but it is clear that it lasted through the entire decade of the 1930s and into the 1940s. And it ended with yet another crisis.

Up and Back Down

The programs of the New Deal definitely had an impact on the economy. By 1937, GDP was back up to 88 percent of pre-crash levels, and the stock market had rebounded somewhat. More importantly, unemployment had dropped back down to 15 percent—still way too high, but significantly lower

Opposite: *President Roosevelt's 1936 campaign button didn't mince words. The vast majority of Americans seemed to agree.*

than it had been when Roosevelt took office in 1933. During Roosevelt's first term, the economy grew at an annual rate of 9 to 10 percent. The plan was working.

The presidential election of 1936 was widely regarded as a referendum on the New Deal. Roosevelt's Republican opponent, Alf Landon, promised to continue the programs of the New Deal as well, but he assured the public that he would do so without running a deficit—an aspect of the New Deal that conservatives took issue with. But clearly, even the Republican Party realized that it would be political suicide to suggest gutting the New Deal program entirely. Voters left no doubt about their approval of the program. They reelected the president in a landslide. He won over 60 percent of the popular vote and all but two states: Maine and Vermont. Democrats also increased what were already large majorities in both houses of Congress. However, not long after the election, the New Deal ran into trouble.

Businesspeople and bankers, mostly Republican, did not share the voters' enthusiasm for the president and his New Deal. Businesspeople were beginning to resent being cast as the greedy bad guys responsible for getting the country into this mess. Also, they felt that government money was being wasted on people who couldn't do anything to help the economy. They were opposed to the country running a deficit to pay for these programs. However, because the Democrats had control of both houses of Congress, there was not much they could do. The Supreme Court, however, was another matter. Four of the nine justices were ideologically opposed to

Roosevelt's programs and consistently opposed his measures; three of the justices usually supported them. The other two were swing votes, but as we saw in chapter 2, the Supreme Court had struck down several key New Deal programs and justices were threatening to do even more damage.

Roosevelt thought that because he had been elected by such a large margin he had a **mandate** from the voters to do what was required to save the New Deal. In February 1937, he proposed dramatic changes to the nation's court system, including adding up to six new justices (who would be chosen by him and likely easily approved by the Democratic Senate) to the Supreme Court, arguing that the justices were overworked. It was no secret that his aim was to fill the court with new, liberal justices who would be friendly to his plans and programs. Not surprisingly, conservatives shrieked at what they called his "court-packing plan."

Many people who supported Roosevelt were disturbed by this. It seemed to a lot of people that the president had become power hungry and was trying to give the president far more power by subverting the balance of power outlined in the US Constitution. On the other hand, it was true that an overwhelming majority of the country supported Roosevelt's programs and did not want the court to overturn them.

In March, the court upheld a minimum wage law, and then in fairly quick succession it upheld the Wagner Act that established the National Labor Relations board and signed off on the Social Security Act—all moves that indicated the court was not (or at least no longer was) deliberately obstructing the president's plan. There no longer seemed much need to pack the court. In one sense, this was a big victory for Roosevelt, and things continued to get better as some of the older justices retired and he was able to appoint new members to the court. However, in another way the whole episode damaged the president politically. Afterwards, conservative elements of the Democratic Party were much more willing to vote against Roosevelt's programs, and often combined with Republican legislators to block New Deal measures.

Roosevelt had also come up with a plan to reorganize the executive branch of the government in order, he said, to make it more efficient. His opponents saw it as yet another power grab. The new coalition of Republicans and conservative Democrats was able to defeat this measure as well, though some changes to the executive branch were made in a less comprehensive bill in 1939.

As if the relationship with his own party wasn't deteriorating fast enough, in the 1938 primary for mid-term congressional elections, Roosevelt actively campaigned against the Democrats who had opposed him. He was unable to prevent any of them from being elected, and his efforts to purge the party of people who opposed him backfired, just making the divide between the president and the conservative wing of his party deeper and more bitter.

However, some of the worst blows to the New Deal were dealt by Roosevelt himself. By 1937, national income had returned to almost the pre-crash levels. In 1929 it was

Even though nothing came of his plans, Roosevelt's suggested changes to the Supreme Court hurt him politically.

$82 billion, then by 1932 it had dropped more than half to $40 billion, but was back up to $72 billion in 1937. Roosevelt and his economic advisors, particularly Treasury Secretary Henry Morgenthau, still wary of running budget deficits, decided that this would be a good time to balance the budget. So Roosevelt began to back off on some of his most effective programs, cutting the WPA in half and laying off 1.5 million workers. The economist John Maynard Keynes called this "an error of optimism." Indeed, within a few weeks of these layoffs

Economic collapse and rising nationalism led to the rise of Hitler and the Nazi Party in Germany.

made to European companies. A similar downward spiral occurred in Europe and soon an estimated forty million workers were without jobs. Germany was particularly hard hit. By 1932, German unemployment had reached 30 percent. Relations between the nations of Europe were still not good, and the economic catastrophe caused countries to pull in and protect their own interests rather than working together for the common good. The United States had already passed strict tariff laws that limited trade with other countries, and Britain soon followed suit.

Economic problems created political ones. In Germany, the country was divided between an extreme right wing, the National Socialist German Worker's Party, or the Nazi Party for short, and extreme left-wing Communist Party. The one thing both parties had in common was an extreme dislike for the other nations of Western Europe as well as the United States, in large part because the conditions imposed by the Allies after World War I had contributed to the economic difficulties the country was experiencing. Germany had been allowed to keep only a small military force, just enough to handle domestic problems, but nothing that could be a threat to other nations. The Allies also took territory Germany had seized before the war and returned it to the countries it had originally belonged to. The German people took all of these measures, but particularly the reparations, as a punishment for the war, a punishment they believed was much too harsh. They felt both desperate and humiliated.

ROOSEVELT AND THE WAR

Had the Great Depression been the only crisis Franklin Roosevelt had to deal with, he would still be considered one of America's greatest leaders. But his leadership in World War II was historic, too. Roosevelt began working closely with the European Allies even before the United States entered the war in 1941. He was elected to a third term (the first and only time a US president has been elected three times) at least in part because the nation

Franklin Roosevelt, Winston Churchill, and Joseph Stalin met in Yalta in 1945 to make decisions about the post-World War II world.

trusted him to lead them through the brewing military crisis as skillfully as he had led them through the economic one.

After gradually convincing the American public of the necessity of involvement in World War II, President Roosevelt took an active role in planning strategy for the war. He was particularly involved in planning the D-Day invasion to liberate France from the Nazi occupation.

Roosevelt was a strong proponent of the United Nations (UN), an international organization designed to promote the political and economic cooperation of the world's nations. He hoped to lay the groundwork for a more peaceful world. Roosevelt died in April 1945, a few months before the end of World War II and before the UN was chartered in October.

When Roosevelt became president, the United States was an isolationist nation, still stinging from World War I and facing the worst economic crisis in its history. When he died, he left the nation a global superpower both economically and politically.

been more isolationist than not, but after World War I, many people were arguing that US involvement in World War I had been not "to make the world safe for democracy," as the slogan had it at that time, but to enrich bankers and businesspeople who had investments in the European **munitions** industry. Convincing the American population to join yet another war in Europe was going to be a tough sell.

Roosevelt realized that the United States would almost certainly not be able to stay out of the conflict, and even before war was declared in Europe, he had tried to prepare the nation. In a speech in 1937, he painted a dire picture of not only what was going on in Europe but also what the consequences might be if the United States did nothing. He explained that innocent countries were being invaded and that "the very foundations of civilization are seriously threatened." He went on to make it clear that the United States would not be able to forever avoid the consequences of what was happening in the rest of the world, saying:

> "*If those things come to pass in other parts of the world, let no one imagine that America will escape, that America may expect mercy … If those days come there will be no safety by arms, no help from authority, no answer in science. The storm will rage till every flower of culture is trampled and all human beings are leveled in a vast chaos.*"

Even with this dramatic oratory, the public still took some convincing. After all, President Woodrow Wilson had argued that by coming to the aid of European nations in World War I, America was helping to forge a world in which the strong could no longer terrorize the weak, and the strong terrorizing the weak was exactly what was happening again. It hardly seemed like a worthwhile effort to get involved once more.

Public opinion did gradually change. As Americans read more and more news articles, and saw newsreel footage of the atrocities the Germans were committing, they began to realize that they needed to intervene. It was clear not only that Hitler and his war machine were unlikely to spare the United States, but that it would be morally unacceptable to sit by and not help the nations he was already invading. By 1939, a majority of Americans favored getting rid of the Neutrality Act, and it was repealed in November of that year. Some restrictions remained in place, but America could now sell arms and grant credit for arms purchases to nations that were at war.

Arsenal of Democracy

By 1940, the German army was bent on taking over the entire continent of Europe. France fell to the Nazis in the spring and on June 4, the British military was forced to abandon most of its tanks and artillery when the German army forced them to retreat across the English Channel at Dunkirk.

AIR POWER

Though planes were used as bombers, fighters, and for reconnaissance in World War I, that war was fought primarily with trench warfare, a land-based type of fighting in which armies dug deep ditches to protect soldiers and defend territory from there. By World War II, planes had become faster, could fly higher, and pilots could communicate with other planes and people on the ground by radio. Airplanes were used extensively in massive bombing raids, as well as for fighting and reconnaissance.

Both the Allies and the Axis powers worked hard throughout the war to gain superiority in the air. They developed new aircraft, air-fighting techniques, and technologies—such as RADAR and bombsights—to increase the effectiveness of air attacks. By the end of World War II, pilots had gone from flying prop planes in dog fights to flying jet airplanes.

This race for new technologies for the air war spurred nations on both sides of the conflict to increase their industrialization in order to build and design better planes. This was a major contributor to the industrial boom that ended the Great Depression.

This B-17 bomber helped change the way modern war is fought.

It was clear that the Allies needed help. In December 1940, Roosevelt, just having been elected to an unprecedented third term, gave a fireside chat in which he declared that the United States must become "the arsenal of democracy." His plan, which became the Lend-Lease Program, was to supply Allies with guns, ships, planes, food—whatever they needed—to fight the Nazis. However, because countries could not afford to pay for the enormous amount of money for the supplies, the United States would lend them the materials, with no expectation that they would ever repay. After World War I, the United States had drastically reduced the size of its armed forces. In 1939, the US Army had roughly 180,000 soldiers and was ranked nineteenth in the world in size, so in addition to providing weapons for Europe, the United States needed to build up its own military in order, at the very least, to be in a position to defend itself if that should become necessary.

All these weapons and supplies had to be manufactured, and that meant more jobs. Lots more jobs. As US factories began to churn out war materials, the economy finally began to pull out of its decade-long slump. In 1941, unemployment dropped below 10 percent for the first time since 1929. In December 1941, Japan bombed Pearl Harbor, an American naval base in Hawaii territory (Hawaii did not become a state until 1959), and the United States declared war on Japan, finally entering World War II. A few days later, Germany declared war on the United States and the US responded by declaring war on Germany. By 1942, unemployment had

337
K

5

The Legacy of the Great Depression and the New Deal

The Great Depression left scars on the American people that still exist today, and the New Deal changed both the way Americans think about the world and the landscape of US politics. The onset of World War II made many New Deal programs unnecessary and certainly eliminated any need for additional economic stimulus programs. But the Great Depression, how Americans coped with it, and what the government did to mitigate the damage fundamentally changed the nation.

A Totally New View

The quarter century after the beginning of World War II was the most prosperous period in United States history to date, and not only the extent but the durability of that prosperity

Opposite: *After World War II, Americans entered an extended period of as-yet unequalled prosperity.*

was in large part due to the changes made during the New Deal. The five years between 1933 and 1938 saw more changes in society and its institutions than any other period in history. Even today, scholars still discuss and debate the various effects of the New Deal and look to it for ideas about what to do (and what to avoid) when facing new economic crises.

Before the New Deal, the federal government played a very small role in the economy of the nation and in the lives of its citizens. That is not to say it played no role—the Federal Reserve was created in 1913 and the Federal Trade Commission in 1914—but there was very little regulation of business or the economy, and the government did next to nothing for individuals. No one expected it to. The doctrine that individuals were responsible for their own fate was deeply embedded in the American psyche. There was an equally ingrained economic orthodoxy: the belief that in times of scarcity the prudent action for the government was to balance budgets and reduce spending. It made a certain kind of sense, particularly if one makes the mistake of imagining the federal government as just a larger version of a household. The programs of the New Deal put a large and permanent dent in this belief. Despite the fact that the New Deal did not go far enough fast enough, the success of its programs did convince most economists that government spending is not only an effective but an often-necessary means of stimulating the economy during downturns.

But as we saw in the last chapter, the New Deal did not end the Great Depression. It took the much larger economic stimulus of producing supplies for World War II to do that. So how did the New Deal have such a significant long-term effect?

Security

It's easy to get caught up in all the details of the many initiatives—the alphabet soup—of the New Deal, and lose sight of the larger goals of the program. Essentially, the New Deal was an effort to more equally distribute the social, political, and economic benefits of capitalism among the citizens of the nation. In that regard, it was a success, but it also provided something else the nation had never had before: economic security. For individuals this means a safety net that offers some protection against job loss, disability, and inevitable old age. It means the security of knowing that if you put your money in the bank, that money will be there when you come back for it. It means that union members have a means of holding employers accountable for obeying labor laws. It means that employers have to pay a minimum wage, and a forty-hour workweek is standard. It means that, thanks to the Home Owner's Loan Corporation established in 1933, millions of Americans who might have lost their homes in the Great Depression were able to keep them, and home ownership increased from 40 percent of the population in the 1920s to 70 percent by the 1990s.

The benefits were not just for individuals, however. Banking reforms benefitted businesses too, and businesses

HEALTH CARE: A LONG WAIT

When Frances Perkins accepted the job as secretary of labor under President Roosevelt, she had an ambitious agenda of social reform that she intended to complete before she left office. She accomplished everything on her list save one item: health care. The notion that all Americans should have access to affordable health care has been around for a long time, but universal health care has been surprisingly hard to achieve in the United States.

At some point there were proposals to add national health insurance to the Social Security bill, but the American Medical Association (AMA) was

Providing health care for all Americans has proven to be one of the United States' greatest challenges.

strongly opposed to the idea. Unwilling to risk the ire of the AMA, Roosevelt dropped health care reform from the plan. That wasn't the last of it, though. In the 1940s, organized labor backed the idea of national health insurance. A national insurance program funded through social security payroll taxes was proposed but never made it into law. Because of public sympathy for the elderly, the AMA was unable to block the creation in 1965 of Medicare—a national insurance program for Americans over sixty-five years old—but the rest of the population was still waiting.

In the 1990s, President Bill Clinton's administration tried to implement a national health care plan, but it too failed, again primarily because of resistance from the medical and insurance industries. Then in 2010, after incredible political maneuvering, President Barack Obama signed the Affordable Care Act into law, creating something close to universal health care. However, the plan was met with a great deal of resistance from Republicans in Congress, and in 2017, the Republican majority in Congress moved to repeal it.

socialist overhaul of the nation, its measures served more to save capitalism from its own internal weaknesses than to damage it. With only minor exceptions, such as the TVA, no major state-owned businesses came out of the New Deal. Roosevelt saved capitalism from itself, even as he saved the citizens from the worst excesses of capitalism.

When President Roosevelt took office in 1933 and was immediately faced with the imminent collapse of the banking system, he could have had the government take over the entire financial system—and many of his advisors thought this would have been the safest bet at that point. Or he could have created a national bank that would have eventually driven the weaker, privately owned banks out of business. Other people—primarily owners of large banks centered around Wall Street and other major financial centers—urged him to relax the few existing restrictions on banks and allow mergers and consolidations, thus creating a highly concentrated private banking industry run by just a few dozen extremely powerful institutions. Instead, he resisted both extremes and left the banking system varied and local, but separated commercial banks from investment banks and created the FDIC to protect commercial deposits (up to a certain amount that has increased over the years). It was a brilliant compromise between regulation and free markets, between government protection and government control. Even before the Depression, bank failures were common—hundreds failed every year. After 1933, the yearly number of bank failures was closer to ten. These measures cost the taxpayers virtually

The Tennessee Valley Authority (TVA) was one of Roosevelt's first New Deal programs, and it still exists today.

nothing and member banks very little, yet stabilized one of the most volatile parts of the economic system.

Lessons Learned

As some of the protections of the New Deal were weakened, the nation got a sharp reminder of the fragility of capitalism. In 2008, the United States came frighteningly close to another Great Depression. Lax oversight of the financial industry, reckless lending, and a risky practice of making high-risk mortgages and then pooling those mortgages in a misguided attempt to lower the risk led to a severe banking crisis. Lehman Brothers, one of the world's largest banks,

It was the first time since the Great Depression that so much government intervention had been needed or used, and it's hard to imagine how any of it could have been done without the experiences and example of the New Deal.

Still Struggling

While the New Deal provided lasting benefits for the economy, it did not prove as beneficial to many of the woes of democracy. After initially doing little for blacks, the New Deal did come around, and African Americans saw some progress during the 1930s, thanks in part to the efforts of the NAACP and the Communist Party pushing for more inclusion of blacks in New Deal programs and for more union membership and fairer representation within unions. But at the end of the Depression, discrimination still existed both in government and private industry, and when whites had returned to full employment, blacks still struggled to find jobs. It would be some more years before Jim Crow laws were challenged and the government began to make a serious effort to address the many injustices done to African Americans over the years.

As we saw in chapter 2, in order to keep enough support from Southern and conservative Democrats, Roosevelt often traded progress for blacks for votes for his programs. However, it became increasingly clear that many Democrats and New Deal supporters were very sympathetic to the cause of black Americans, and they prepared the groundwork for

ECONOMIC AND ENVIRONMENTAL JUSTICE

Most of the programs of the New Deal were innovative, but perhaps none was quite as ambitious as the Tennessee Valley Authority (TVA), a federally owned corporation designed to use government funding and expertise to modernize and boost the economy of the Tennessee River Valley. Roosevelt envisioned the TVA as "a corporation clothed with the power of government but possessed of the flexibility and initiative of a private enterprise." In 1933, the Tennessee River Valley was in bad shape. The river frequently flooded and navigating it was difficult and dangerous. The soil had been depleted and eroded by poor farming techniques, and timber harvesting had deforested much of the area. Many of the people who lived in the region were poor, ill, and few had electricity in their homes. Malaria outbreaks were common.

Roosevelt was interested in conservation as well as economic justice, and saw the TVA as a way to address environmental and economic issues in the same big program. The TVA not only built dams to improve navigation, control flooding, and provide hydroelectric power, but it also replanted forests, improved habitats for wildlife, and trained farmers in how to improve crop yields and take better care of the soil. Bringing electricity to the area attracted more industry, which provided desperately needed jobs for the people living there. The TVA was and still is a government-owned utility. Today it provides electric power to almost nine million people in parts of seven southeastern states.

later progress. The number of black Americans in government was still small, but larger than it ever had been before. Roosevelt appointed the first black federal judge, William Hastie. Several New Deal agencies had advisors for "negro affairs" on their staffs. In 1936, Roosevelt appointed educator and civil rights activist Mary McLeod Bethune as director of the Division of Negro Affairs for the National Youth Administration. Bethune often led informal meetings of the African Americans in government, and this group came to be known as the "Black Cabinet." Bethune became a close friend and advisor to both Franklin and Eleanor Roosevelt.

African Americans made other gains as well. In 1935, the Maryland Court of Appeals ordered the University of Maryland to admit blacks to its law school. (Because this was many years before the landmark 1954 *Brown versus the Board of Education* ruling, which found separate schools unconstitutional, the university had the option of creating a separate but equal law school for blacks. However, this would have been much too expensive, so the university began admitting blacks.) In 1936, a large coalition of African American civil rights, labor, and religious groups joined together to form the National Negro Congress (NNC), an organization designed to work toward economic recovery for blacks as well as whites. The NNC had a loose affiliation with the Communist Party and did not survive the **Cold War**. However, it represented a new and vigorous political mobilization of African Americans, which outlasted the NNC.

The New Deal turned African Americans into a reliable voting bloc for the Democratic Party.

Different Parties

The New Deal brought African Americans into the Democratic Party and, while not coming even close to giving them social and political justice, it did give them a voice and a place in the political community. And if New Deal Democrats changed things slightly for the African American community, African Americans changed things enormously for the Democratic Party. As we saw in chapter 3, blacks who had traditionally supported Republicans—the party of Abraham Lincoln—became reliably Democratic voters starting in the 1930s. When the Depression hit blacks especially hard and Hoover did nothing to help, they, like most Americans, turned their hopes to the Democratic Party.

Black politicians also saw opportunities in the strengthening Democratic Party. In 1932, Arthur Mitchell of Illinois became the first black Democrat elected to the House of Representatives, and other black politicians would follow him to the Democratic Party. Only 5 percent of African Americans to serve in Congress between 1929 and 2007 were Republicans.

The Democrats' New Deal coalition, made up of blue-collar workers, union members, immigrants, and blacks, fell apart somewhat in later years as the Democratic Party shifted its attention from the concerns of the working class, much of the South became Republican, and blue-collar workers became more socially and fiscally conservative. However, even today the Democratic Party is clearly seen as the party of big government, supporting more spending on social and domestic programs and more help for those at the bottom of the socioeconomic spectrum, while the Republican Party is largely seen as supportive of business and higher income groups.

Different Attitudes

The New Deal not only convinced many economists that the government had a role in managing the economy, but it changed the way Americans viewed their government as well. Before the Great Depression, Americans did not expect the federal government to play a significant role in their lives. After the New Deal, very few Americans were opposed to all government intervention in the economy or society, and programs like social security are still very popular. Though many Americans in the twenty-first century have concerns about whether or not the government will be able to pay benefits by the time they need them, there is widespread support for the program. Sixty-seven percent of Americans believe that protecting the social security program should be a top priority of the government, according to a 2015 survey by the Pew Research Center—and it's not just social security. Americans by a wide margin support a variety of social programs. According to a Pew survey conducted in 2013, after the Great Recession, sympathy for the poor and support for social programs surged.

Today, social programs do seem to work. According to a 2014 analysis by the Pew Research organization, the poverty rate in the United States was 14.5 percent. Without a government-funded supplemental nutrition program that rate would be 17.1 percent—another eight million people in poverty. According to the same survey, without social security the poverty rate of Americans sixty-five years old and older would jump from 14.6 percent to almost 53 percent.

A New Kind of President

Prior to Franklin Roosevelt, presidents were typically expected to ensure that the nation's laws were "faithfully executed," but did not by and large play a big role in crafting legislation. Roosevelt changed that. He pushed through

GLOSSARY

capitalism An economic and political system in which business and industry are owned by private individuals rather than the government.

Cold War The period in the second half of the twentieth century in which the conflict between the Soviet Union and the United States was limited to threats, propaganda, and supporting rival factions, but never came to direct war.

communism An economic and political system in which all property is publicly owned.

default To fail to repay a loan.

deficit The state in a budget, such as that of a government, in which expenditures exceed revenue.

Fascism A philosophy or form of government that privileges authoritarianism, nationalism, and often racism.

Federal Reserve The banking authority in the United States that implements monetary policy, such as setting and adjusting interest rates.

gross domestic product (GPD) The value of goods and services produced by a country.

levee A dike or embankment built to prevent a river from flooding.

lynch To murder, typically by a mob, usually by hanging.

mandate The authority to carry out a policy agenda, thought to be given by voters when an official win elections by large margins.

munitions Ammunition, weapons, and equipment used for war.

nationalism An extreme form of patriotism that elevates one country's culture and policies over those of all other countries or peoples.

nativism The practice or policy of privileging the interests of people who were born in a country over the interests of immigrants.

neutrality Impartiality in a conflict, such as a war.

Reconstruction The period following the US Civil War in which the former Confederate States were controlled and reestablished by the federal government.

reparations Financial or other compensation made to the victors in war by the defeated nation or nations.

secularism Lack of interest in or affiliation with religion or religious beliefs and practices.

suffrage The right to vote (also known as franchise).

tariff A tax levied on imports or exports.

CHRONOLOGY

November 11, 1918 World War I ends.

October 29, 1929 Black Tuesday, US stock market crashes.

November 8, 1932 Franklin D. Roosevelt is elected president of the United States.

March 5, 1933 President Roosevelt orders a four-day bank holiday.

March 12 Roosevelt delivers his first fireside chat.

March 21 The Civilian Conservation Corps (CCC) is created.

May 18 The Tennessee Valley Authority (TVA) is created.

June 16 Congress passes legislation authorizing the Public Works Administration (PWA) and the Federal Deposit Insurance Corporation (FDIC).

June 6, 1934 The Securities and Exchange Commission is established.

May 6, 1935 The Works Progress Administration (WPA) is established.

May 27 The Supreme Court declares the National Industrial Recovery Act unconstitutional.

July 5 Congress establishes the National Labor Relations Board.

August 14 The Social Security Act is signed into law.

February 17, 1936 The Supreme Court upholds the Tennessee Valley Authority.

February 5, 1937 Roosevelt announces his plan to add six justices to the Supreme Court.

June 25, 1938 The Fair Labor Standards Act establishes a minimum wage and maximum work hours.

September 1, 1939 World War II begins.

December 8, 1941 The United States declares war on Japan and enters World War II.

FURTHER INFORMATION

Books

Bryson, Bill. *One Summer: America, 1927.* New York: Anchor, 2014.

Freedman, Russell. *Eleanor Roosevelt: A Life of Discovery.* New York: Houghton Mifflin, 1997.

Phelan, Matt. *Storm in the Barn.* New York: Candlewick, 2009.

Websites

Library of Congress: Voices from the Dust Bowl

https://www.loc.gov/collections/todd-and-sonkin-migrant-workers-from-1940-to-1941/about-this-collection

Audio recordings and images document the everyday lives of people during the Great Depression.

"Protectionism in the Interwar Year Period"

https://history.state.gov/milestones/1921-1936/protectionism

This website offers an explanation of tariffs and protectionism during the interwar period, compiled by the Office of the Historian of the US Department of State.

Videos

Public Broadcasting System: Back in Time: *The Grapes of Wrath*

http://videos.oeta.tv/video/2365373523/

This thirty-minute video looks at the historical realities behind the novel.

Public Broadcasting System: The Great Depression

https://www.youtube.com/watch?v=IQ_lizW5zSI

This fifty-five-minute presentation on the Great Depression includes period footage and commentary by people who lived at the time.

Organizations

Frances Perkins Center

http://francesperkinscenter.org/life-new

This site is dedicated to preserving the political legacy of Frances Perkins.

Franklin Delano Roosevelt Presidential Library and Museum

https://fdrlibrary.org

This is the official website of the Franklin Delano Roosevelt Presdential Library and Museum.

Metropolitan Museum of Art: Walker Evans

http://www.metmuseum.org/toah/hd/evan/hd_evan.htm

This website shows part of the Heilbrunn Timeline of Art History, a selection of essays, links, and information about Walker Evans.

SELECTED BIBLIOGRAPHY

American Presidency Project. "Hoover's Radio Address to the Nation on Unemployment Relief," October 18, 1931. Accessed October 5, 2016, http://www.presidency.ucsb.edu/ws/?pid=22855.

Belson, Ken. "Apples for a Nickel, and Plenty of Empty Seats." *New York Times*. January 6, 2009. Retrieved October 10, 2016, http://www.nytimes.com/2009/01/07/sports/baseball/07depression.html.

Brinkley, Alan. *American History: A Survey, Volume II* (9th edition). New York: McGraw Hill, 1995.

Bryson, Bill. *One Summer: America, 1927*. New York: Anchor, 2014.

Kennedy, David M. *Freedom from Fear: The American People in Depression and War 1929–1945*. New York: Oxford University Press, 1999.

Kreitner, Richard. "August 26, 1920: The 19th Amendment Goes Into Effect, Granting Women the Right To Vote." *The Nation*, August 26, 2015. Accessed October 10, 2016, https://www.

thenation.com/article/august-26-1920-the-19th-amendment-is-ratified-granting-women-the-vote.

Krugman, Paul. "New Deal Economics." *New York Times*, November 8, 2008. Accessed November 9, 2016, http://krugman.blogs.nytimes.com/2008/11/08/new-deal-economics.

Long Legacy Project. "Share Our Wealth." Accessed November 10, 2016, http://www.hueylong.com/programs/share-our-wealth.php.

Rauchway, Eric. *The Great Depression and the New Deal: A Very Short Introduction*. Oxford, UK: Oxford University Press, 2008.

Steinbeck, John. *The Grapes of Wrath*. New York: Penguin, 1939.

United States House of Representatives, History Art and Archives. "World War I and the Great Migration." Accessed November 17, 2016, http://history.house.gov/Exhibitions-and-Publications/BAIC/Historical-Essays/Temporary-Farewell/World-War-I-And-Great-Migration.

United States Social Security Administration. "Historical Background and Development of Social Security." Accessed November 17, 2016, https://www.ssa.gov/history/briefhistory3.html.

Virginia Commonwealth University: The Social Welfare History Project. "Stock Market Crash of October 1929." Accessed October 2, 2016, http://socialwelfare.library.vcu.edu/eras/

great-depression/beginning-of-great-depression-stock-market-crash-of-october-1929.

Walsh, Kenneth. "The Most Consequential Elections in History: Franklin Delano Roosevelt and the Election of 1932." *US News and World Report*, September 10, 2008. Accessed November 15, 2016, http://www.usnews.com/news/articles/2008/09/10/the-most-consequential-elections-in-history-franklin-delano-roosevelt-and-the-election-of-1932.

Ward, Geoffrey C., and Ken Burns. *Jazz: A History of America's Music*. New York: Alfred A. Knopf, 2000.

INDEX

Page numbers in **boldface** are illustrations. Entries in **boldface** are glossary terms.

ABOUT THE AUTHOR

Avery Elizabeth Hurt is the author of many books for children and young adults, mostly about social studies and science. She has long been fascinated by how history tends to repeat itself—with variations. And she has a great deal of faith in humans to learn from that history.